SPLENDOUR

SPLENDOUR

P.GOPICHAND/P.NAGASUSEELA

PARTRIDGE

A Penguin Random House Company

To order additional copies of this book, contact
Partridge India
000 800 10062 62
www.partridgepublishing.com/india
orders.india@partridgepublishing.com

CONTENTS

Foreword

The creator not only created this wonderful world but also bestowed on human beings to see, feel and reflect the wonderful things in our works of art. In the passage of time we come across various situations and incidents that make us respond. Our spontaneous responses to our festivals, rituals, events, problems, calamities, changes in nature came out in the form of short poems. These poems contain a scene or an incident to the reader. Truths and realities of life parade in the short poems which makes the reader feel splendorous experience. We wish that our efforts in making this small book of verse will make the readers feel and experience the strong vibrations of life whenever they glance at them. Simple words and common images are used by us so that it can be reached to all ages of readers. Human feelings are universal. So the appeal is also universal. We thank the poets in India and also abroad for encouraging us and suggesting us to bring out these poems in the form of a book for the wide circulation.

P.Gopichand & P.Nagasuseela

CREATIVE WRITING

Oh! Dear Goddesss Muse
Roses bloomed in your garden
Grand is our poet's touch

    Colours in our life
    Like rainbow hues amuse us
    Let Muse fuse them all

        Creative Writing
        Sprouts so many wonder lands
        Authors are jugglers

            Fusion of Fine Arts
            Diffuses Rainbows in life
            Heart throbs for creation

Jana Gana Mana

Freedom bells echo
Our Jana gana mana
Alerts our conscience

From generations
Song Jana gana mana
Makes us think awhile

Wings of duty float
Caste, creed, culture no barrier
To serve our own land

Drenched with emotion
So rhythmic our anthem
Rouses devotion

VANDE MATHARAM

Vande Matharam
A symbol of new sunrise
Great gift to Indians

      Unites our hearts
      As rivers merge into seas
      India glows well

            Breath of millions
            Echo is the freedom spirit
            All through the seasons

                  Our National Anthem
                  Sprinkles peace like fresh dew drops
                  Make our country great

LOVE

Love is a feeling
That fills the heart with honey
Beyond all reasons

Love is a rainbow
Bridges many barriers
Proved time and again

Pains and sufferings
Love makes all of them in vain
Restores happiness

Tears and doubts
Like winter fog stay alike
Love dispels them all

Lovers are lucky
Love conquers all our hungers
Humans turn divine

Hopes like creepers grow
Gain strength with passage of time
None can arrest growth

One soul in two forms
As rain drops fuse into streams
Forms only oneself

Love like deep red wine
Appetizer to lead life
Makes our life tasty

Real love brings fair glow
Sprinkles smiles like full moon
Others notice soon

      Love creates dream world
      Like sea surf inexhaustible
      Love tales are not stale

            All cares and concerns
            Shows the fragrance of love
            Kindles hope candles

                  In times of troubles
                  Like gentle ripples in pond
                  Love soothes you unasked

Like lids to eye balls
Love guards all lovers from fears
God's boon to man kind

Time sprinkles changes
Love is beyond all seasons
Remains forever

Like Summer showers
Love a balm to all problems
Breeds courage in heart

All true loving souls
More powerful than atom bombs
God too can't tame love

Love- a rare flower
Blooms suddenly without bud
Never fades away

In love seas dolphins
Sing melodious tunes
Seasoning hard hearts

Daily life triggers
Hot emotions like lava
True love restores peace

Love- a lubricant
Makes the wheels of human life
Run smooth till the end

LIFE

Life a vast ocean
Tears and smiles like ebbs and flows
Come incessantly

Life a big fine fair
Full of hustle and bustle
Till that long silence

We grow many bonds
Like roots they hold us tight
Till we breathe our last

In our life long race
We face many deceits
And soon regain trust

Life is not commerce
Frank trading mars human
Heart makes life pleasant

> For many ages
> Life in a handful of grains
> Misunderstood well

> > Life's pendulum swings
> > Between trust and mistrust points
> > Wisdom dawns at last

> > > Idiots on the earth
> > > Blame us for their shortcomings
> > > They too live with us

Life's long weary way
Has mineral springs somewhere
Time will lead to them

      Life's a grand circus
      Perform the feats cautiously
      Leave the rest to fate

         Hard to read people
         Face isn't the index of mind
         Life time isn't enough

            Life-a giant shadow
            Stays static when you're passive
            Active when you move

FRIENDSHIP

Cast on troubled seas
Friendship saves us from drowning
Like life-boat on earth

  When your bosom aches
  Hot tears roll from friend's eyes
  Friend, a true mirror

    A friend removes wants
    As autumn season provides
    Delight to senses

      Pains of seclusion
      Relieved by friendship balm
      A rare miracle

Friendship like a camel
Carries you through horrid climes
None can replace friend

> Friend gives immense strength
> As mountains brave all weathers
> A shield that guards us

> Pray for friend's safety
> Your friendship train without strain
> Takes you to heaven

> True friends are rare gems
> Precious stones turn pale
> None can buy true friends

NATURE

Ducks in paddy fields
Like waves in the sea they glide
A scene after harvest

Clusters of houses
Like white cranes in serene ponds
Still life delightful

Small red tile houses
Like every grand dawn and dusk
Live close to nature

Yellow coconuts
Like moonlight attract young hearts
Dry tongues make us drink

Tall coconut trees
Like Ganga on Siva's head
Bear water in nuts

Hill chains round our coast
Like links in gold chain
All are similar

Cute red-coloured bricks
Attract like red sun in the morn
Thillana on platform

Small green raw plantains
As kids cling to their mother
Hooked to plant with pride

Weeds strangle water
Like a frog in a snake's mouth
Summer in progress

    Big bark-less trees fell
    Saw many Springs and Summers
    All to dust must turn

        Palm trees waving heads
        Like soldiers guarding farm lands
        Sentries on frontiers

            Hay-stack harvest signs
            Sweat and tears' testimony
            Every year the same

Gloom On all sides spreads
Like ghost-clouds cover the sky
Time changes the tide

Choose the path you like
Guard our Nature till you die
Kids must have future

Clinging to green leaves
Butterflies a feat to eyes
Nature's gift to us

Winter spreads its bed
Dawn and dusk tell us life truth
Bright days are in store

WATER

Oh, Water, water
Wars for drinking rage
All over the world

Let us think for a while
Water, a source of our life
Please don't waste water

Think of the future
A drop will reverse our life
The worse will rule us

Please don't waste in haste
Save green earth with right actions
Earth, a place for love

You are better than ape
Don't rape the green earth
Nurse it carefully

    Water in bottles
    Precious source for modern life
    Competes with money

        Without pure water
        Animals, plants or humans
        Nowhere can be seen

            Save a drop today
            It will save us forever
            Keep nature intact

Rains and Pains

Seasons sprout wishes
Clouds sprinkle hope in farmers
Ploughs the land with glee

Lightening and thunder
Swallow the creeks that bones make
Heart throbs for good yield

Seeds are sown with care
Sweat and rain give life to seed
New shoots trigger dreams

Time breeds great problems
Weeds and pests bring restlessness
Farmer groans in pain

Too many showers
Scanty rain and sudden storms
Paralyze farmer

Power cuts and dried wells
Dry the tears of farmers soon
Crickets morn the loss

Clouds at harvest time
Like cobras frighten farmers
Labour-at cross roads

Rains at harvest time
Like a snake gulping bird's eggs
Heart melts into tears

Cyclones

Philin to Helen
Cyclones threw life out of gear
All crops rest on ground

Flash floods and cyclones
Wash out our dreams, hopes and all plans
Wreak havoc in lives

High hopes rock on swing
Like big sea tide beautiful
Cyclones mar this joy

Gold grains shake with feat
Like cobras hiss in storm-rain
Floods hit farmer's eyes

FLOODS

Floods made us roofless
Like python gulped all our dreams
Life marooned in floods

Knee deep in waters
Like owls groping for shelter
Life is a mirage

Furious flood water
Embracing crops with ghosts' strength
Spoil coiled fields

Men stagnant in floods
Display silent suffering
Pain goes beyond words

GANESH CHATURDHI

'Impediments God'
Steamed sweet ricecakes offerings
Let the year be smooth

Fresh flowers, plants and fruits
Mud-God with all distortions
Strange scent fill the air

All green and ripe fruits
Dishes and cookies accept
Ganesh-success God

Born out of wet mud
Receives all our offerings
Disolves in water

UGADI

Almanac readings
A feed to our hopes and dreams
A rope to pull life

Swinging through problems
Like ants wading through rain-streams
Ugadi gives boosts

Life's sweet and harsh things
Like cactus plants with fine blooms
Looms large before eyes

Ugadi's anvil
Mingles bitter, sweet, and sour
Jingle life's music

Cuckoos on trees
Heralds New Year's arrival
Echoing sweet tunes

Ugadi chutney
Nourishes positive blood
Makes us strong in souls

On Ugadi day
All our Pundits like the seers
Predict year-long things

Ugadi kindles
Unknown spirits in nature
Sprinkles new wishes

SRIRAMA NAVAMI

In Swayamvara
Rama broke Shiva's Dhanush
Sita Rama fused

On Dasarath's wish
Rama like an ideal son
Moved to thick forests

Sita went with Ram
As water from high to low
Followed to forest

In Bhadrachalam
Dry palm leaves shade in Summer
Muse Rama's wedding

SriRama's marriage
In hot Summer afternoon
Delights devotees

On the wedding day
Pearls shower on Sita's head
Happiness to all

On Ram Navami
Cool holy jaggery drink
Kindles our spirits

Rama and Sita
Like water and milk mixed well
Ideal to couples

DEEWALI

Festival of lights
Dear to Hindus, Sikhs, Buddhists
All feel festive glow

Children love Deevali
New clothes and sweets sway their hearts
They toy with crackers

Clay lamps on threshold
Spell the Victory of Good
Warning to evils

A Colourful sight
Sparkles on the horizon
Beckons Deewali

Lights and sounds echoed
The beauty and the beast in us
Both give seasons law

      Lamps are burning bright
      In front of huts and buildings
      Wave to passing wind

            Rockets pierce through air
            Like mushrooms bloom and fade
            Our hearts leap with joy

                  Crackers burst with smoke
                  Spreads heavy thick blanket
                  Giving warmth to hearts

Harvest season ends
Farmers all have gentle smiles
All gains with Food grains

    Tradesmen with new books
    New hopes with colourful blooms
    Devoutly pray to Gods

        Most auspicious day
        Lakshmi from Kshira Sagar
        Spreads riches through lights

            Oil lamps sway with grace
            Crackers start light and sound show
            Joy reflects in hearts

Flowerpots sprinkle sparks
Like dewdrops from petals drop
Grandeur last for long

Rockets spraying sparks
Like comets dance in dark sky
They link earth and sky

Smoke ghosts dance in air
Like fine ballet wonderful
Joy fills our nerves

Our hopes and wishes
Like crackers should give delight
Dream about success

RAMLEELA

Naraka monster
Like winter troubled people
Distress limitless

God in human forms
Krishna and Satyabhama
Waged war on evil

Ten days and ten nights
Like endless sea-waves fought
Lord Krishan got tired

Great Satyabhama
Like the flames of volcano
Rose and killed Naraka

Arrows flew like hawks
They struck him like big cobras
He fell like huge oak

    Happiness broke out
    Crackers and sparkles bloomed full
    Hope and peace restored

        Every year with joy
        Our hearts recall Ramleela
        Deewali spreads mirth

            The young and the old
            With same gusto celebrate
            The triumph of the good

HOLI

Fist full of colours
A splash of rainbow on earth
Made our living smooth

Splash of all colours
Like a rainbow bloomed here
Young and old play smiles

Exhibit colours
Of love, hope and courage
To all our dear ones

Festival of hues
Very dear to young and old
Fuses emotions

THE NEW YEAR

Twelve hours to strike twelve
Day date month and year change
Dream the New Year's range

  All our endeavours
  Like autumn fruits be fruitful
  Sprinkle happiness

    All our wants vanish
    Like mists in winter season
    Contentment prevails

      Our colourful dreams
      Like the hues in the rainbow
      Leave us in delight

Like changing seasons
All passions should bring happiness
Joy should bring ripeness

    Old year dies in pubs
    With dance, drink and friends
    Voices turn hoarse

        Welcome the New Year
        With shouts, greetings and promises
        Young and old feel same

            Resolve to perform
            What you desire, dream or think
            To fulfil your wish

RAKHI

Brother and sister
Like strong creepers entwined well
Rakhi-a sweet bond

Rakhi festival
Fills my heart with confidence
A sweet memory

Stand by me always
The bond wound round your right wrist
Shortens distances

Bonds in fine wrist bands
Seen in the eyes of brothers
An age old custom

Population

Population ghost
Girdles the world like python
Difficult to breathe

>Price hike pierces our heart
>Like sunstroke it affects us
>Life style changes fast

>Population rise
>Triggers issues plentiful
>Like hills remain hard

>Food and jobs scanty
>As rain-fed streams people sprout
>Panic fills our hearts

The old are burden
Like ripe fruits bend tree branches
A sin to live long

Water and air soiled
As trees litter all dry leaves
Population flows

Natural resources
Disappear like wild spirits
Numbers consume much

Observe one or none
Like a plant in a pot grows
Enjoys all the best

Pollution

Tons and tons of garbage
Waste matters in clear waters
Pollutes life on earth

Bulging smoke demon
Choking our life with iron hands
Dark trails every where

Thunders shout aloud
The dangers that are in store
Bleak future a head

Two giant pollutions
E-world and polythine world
Globe is garbage can

FRIENDSHIP DAY

Friendship should last long
Sharing and caring heart-throbs
In coming seasons

Life is one by two
Stand together in all climes
My heart chants your name

All dew drops reflect
Your tender feelings so well
You fill my heart

Your kindness pervades
Like fragrance from rose gardens
Our bond may blossom

May happiness sprout
Between you and me always
Our friendship-unique

I'm your palanquin
You're my honey stored in heart
Our friendship is great

Our hearts throb alike
Our operas echo life
Friendship a sweet tune

Loves to chat with friend
Like a cherry on the cake
Always gives delight

WOMEN'S DAY

Women on the earth
Like candles show us our path
God's grand creation

Women like lemon
Gives nourishment to us all
From our birth to death

Women face problems
For ages like sages-calm
Man-take care of belle

Long saga of tears
With patience in abundance
Women make history

Woman to us all
Nature in miniature
God in flesh and blood

   Labyrinth of sad woes
   All are formal and normal
   Strange is women's world

      Cleans smoke and garbage
      Like winter covers all fine thoughts
      Heart throbs with service

         Owes a lot to her
         A true friend of the whole world
         Replica of God

TEACHER'S DAY

Laying paths for us
Architects of our future
Teacher-great builder

Teachers are mile stones
Like light house guiding students
Changing society

Teacher a rare gift
Like load star guides us always
Makes us better souls

Builds our character
Like a bee gathers honey
Teaches life skills well

VALENTINE'S DAY

You reflect in me
My heart echoes your voice
My breath chants your name

    You carved your image
    With deeds and actions gentle
    Love is immortal

        Love makes all pleasant
        Evil too loses itself
        Love sooths all pains

            Love flutters in heart
            As flowers bloom in our garden
            All are season's fools

AIDS DAY

Flesh triggers passions
Like a volcano erupts
Sure is destruction

In a weak moment
Thoughtless acts mar our virtues
Future fills with pain

Youth hunt for pleasure
Crave for free life like a bird
Death hunts them always

AIDS Day every year
Reminds us of virtues lost
Needs act with caution

ACID ATTACKS

Lost a precious eye
Soft feelings disappeared
Horror smears remain

Beauty brought much pain
Devil in man left a mark
Thoughtless act killed her

Tender skin melted
Heartless man caused great pain
She swings in coma

Failed in life's exam
Trauma haunts her like hell-hounds
Men left her no peace

Samson

Eyeless in Gaza
Like breathing corpse Samson spent
Miserable life

Chosen by the God
Deliverer of his men
Hopes in all vanished

Dalila with wiles
Like bees attract to flowers
Drew Samson's secret

Wild Samson blinded
Chained to his thoughts and actions
Crushed by strong remourse

Old Manoa came
Heavy with age and suffering
To free his Samson

> Samson rejected
> Like some birds migrate in Seasons
> He to his thoughts clung

> Dalila's request
> Like dry desert yielded none
> She vanished in pain

> Harapha the great
> As tides in the sea challenged
> Samson to conflict

Dagon's solemn feast
As colourful as rainbow
Samson source of joy

Samson pulled pillars
As trees in storms uprooted
Philistines lay dead

Timeless to lament
Samson as winter left quite
Gained freedom from all

Tomb by Manoa
Like memory of Spring yields
Happy memories

GANDHI

Like Gowtham Buddha
Gandhi preached non-violence
Brought freedom to us

Gandhi in loin cloth
As dove stands always for peace
Caught the whole world

Bullets pierced his heart
'Hey Ram'-flowed out from Gandhi
Violence was silenced

Violence was frozen
Cobra's venom no effect
Divine smile was fixed

Think for a moment
When peace is killed by violence
Think of our martyrs

      Gandhi's ashram life
      Seasons body, mind and soul
      Binds man to nature

            Gandhi's war for peace
            Gave rise to many movements
            All over the world

                  Spin thread and earn bread
                  He spun thread all through his life
                  Gandhi a model

Like a true sadhu
He ate nuts and drank goat's milk
Minimised his needs

Through non-violence
Gandhi in South Africa
Became peace master

Gandhi in London
Led an exemplary life
A matter of pride

Cottage industry
Backbone to Mother India
Proposed by Gandhi

MICHAEL JACKSON

With his sprightly dance
Took the whole world in his stride
His name left him pride

Built houses in hearts
Left a fragrance of grace here
A divine wonder

Spoke Cosmic language
Gods demons and humans swayed
In good harmony

Stone tells where he lies
Dance smell his presence always
Binds hearts with rhythm

LUST

Swirling tongues of lust
Give birth to pain and suffering
Trauma painted in psyche

Unknown danger knocks us
Removing innocent veil
Trails of damage lost in time's track

No noose for lust
Lust pest modern threat
Lust for news-a great nuisance

Modern man's only act
Harvesting crimes in tons
Human values become mirage

CORRUPTION

Corruption monster
Sucks nations vitality
Decay is definite

      Every cell of man
      Addicted to corruption
      Emits evil acts

           Law, Justice and God
           All bought with filthy money
           Humanity lost

                Lands, islands and seas
                Thirst for luxuries mars peace
                Bleak is our future

YOGA

Air is everywhere
Like water a common thing
Regulates our life

Inhale and exhale
Like day and night regular
Looks easy but tough

All ailments vanish
Like vapour without knowledge
When breath is perfect

Sit and regulate
Like a crane in still waters
Peace prevails in us

Concentrate on breath
Like a cloud you glide on sky
Your pours fill with joy

      Thoughts rush through our minds
      Like houseflies on rainy day
      To clear them is hard

            Allow thoughts to run
            Like flash floods very soon calm down
            Thoughtless state remains

                  We see lights parade
                  Like the sun beams sharp and fast
                  We pass through strange worlds

Vertical we rise
Like a fountain beautiful
Sheer joy escalates

    Settlers on lotus
    Like birds all wants fly away
    Heaven comes to you

        Tensions fly from you
        Like hunters' horn dispels birds
        Yoga extends life

            Yoga brings order
            Like Nature levels evil
            Life is made divine

PEACE

Blasts miss our heart beat
Like dolls from shelf fell humans
Scars scare all species

     All beliefs silenced
     Storms of passions left debris
     Life swings in crutches

          Mad brains bring havoc
          Like devils' dance terror sprout
          Tension fits seize us

               Human values lost
               Like treasures plundered by thugs
               Monsters live on earth

HERBS

Plants and roots are herbs
With man all diseases grew
Seasons aid them well

Charka laid the path
The world of Ayurved bloomed
Wonder to the modern world

Mothers knew all herbs
They are doctors at our home
Make balms for all aches

Nature, man's mother
Bestows life and energy
Don't destroy mother

OIL SPILL

The big seas soiled well
Oil spills diminish life
Haste always breeds waste

Oil from the deep core
Spill deep seas suddenly
Extingiush our lives

Oil boils our lives
We thrive or sink on oil costs
Oil spills kill us

When oil spoil our seas
Media cries it out loud
All is lost in time

SEASONS

Journey to dream-scapes
Forlorn cuckoos symphony
Heart craves for fine spring

Weeds strangle water
Like a frog in a snake's mouth
Summer in progress

Fresh fruits in basket
Autumn's full store at hand
Nature's at its best

Winter spreads its bed
Dawn and dusk tell us life's truth
Bright days are in store

OLD AGE

The old guide us well
Like the sun throw light on things
Their knowledge is wealth

Learning has no age
Like the sea waves be busy
Play life-game with joy

Their rich experience
Like Nature's treasures vital
They are guiding force

Crossing stressful paths
To cope up with currents of life
Tough task in old age

CELL PHONES

Tender baby plays
Devil that misleads always
Cells crave for cell phone

Cell phones are hell phones
From filthy rich to paupers
Talk on phone all day

Solitude's sole tool
To share all our joys and woes
Round the globe all the time

Cell Phone a menace
Like salt use it properly
Don't use while at work

Far away from home
All relations-a mirage
With out a cell phone

Cell phones stink with sins
Satan took the form of cell
Settle in this world

Cell bridges man
One to many or many to one
Breeds tensions, peace

A cell phone I need
With ring tunes of nightingales
To bridge tender hearts

Father

Friend, guide and mentor
Creator and protector
All rolled into one

Sons rebellious
Fathers bridling sons always
Position matters

Friend, guide and mentor
Creator and protector
All rolled into one

Fathers doubt their sons
They know the roads not taken
Relation ships sail

Dad, Papa or Pa
An authority figure
Replica of love

Knows about our needs
Gives us his support through out
Soul of family

My Dad after God
Provides each and everything
None can replace him

Ugly or handsome
Rich or poor, sober or rude
Father is father

INTERNET

Log to internet
Wriggling like a fish on land
To enter new world

Caught in channels net
Like fly in cobweb wriggling
A lone tree in fall

We sent mails through net
Like swift as the wild panther
Cold is their reply

Internet a fad
Like the big sees eternal
Always exciting

DREAMS

Our dreams unify
The body, mind and spirit
Discovers our self

Rare or recurring
Common or spiritual dreams
Man lives in dream land

A means to explore
To get better perspective
Of our self and soul

Dream-a form of wish
Touch stone of character
Trumpet of conscience

To accomplish things
Dream it, desire, plan and act
Get the life you wish

> Be a good dreamer
> Dream of your goals and future
> Achieve by hard work

> Dreams mesmerize us
> Keep all our worries away
> Fulfill our desires

> Dreams, dreams, Silly dreams
> Senseless dreams, funny dreams
> World felt in our dream

School

School life gives a boost
Teachers teach from their heart
This is not a boast

All the world's a school
All men and women teachers
Life-a big exam

Temple of learning
Key to our style of living
Gateway to earning

Our life a big school
lessons at every stage taught
Those who like will learn

BEAUTY

Huge clouds like dark locks
Silver lining in contrast
A beautiful sight

Beauty in nature
Duty in life and living
Makes the world happy

Sun rise and sun set
Two eternal beauties in sky
Source of joy to all

Your beauty your foe
Face boldly time's challenges
Don't be self centered

Candles

The days of future
Like candles on Christmas eve
Glow with happiness

Lit the rare candles
Of Love, Hope, Peace and Courage
Through out the New Year

Ring out your sadness
With the candles of Joy and Grace
Ring in Cheerfulness

Let us dispel dark
With the candles of Prudence
Knowledge and Wisdom

ANGER

Thoughts eat up our years
Ants of anger consume us
From head to heal

History of kingdoms
Pages written by anger
Witness of the past

Let us face others'
Anger and indifference
With understanding

Lost soul in anger
Sold values to weakness
Remained all alone

Stupid arguments
Shoots all our rage and anger
We have to pay high

Anger-a stone cast
Straight into a bee hive
Face consequences

Let us not look back
In great anger and vengeance
All grief will be brief

Stings sprout our anger
Anger fuels vendetta
Great souls forgive all

Appreciation

Praise the thing you like
Like cuckoo sing the merit
Showers joy to parched hearts

Clap your hands with mirth
Like rain brings joy to our kids
Lit hope in artists

Hurl the words of praise
Like flowers showered at God
Be kind to all arts

Need not praise the great
A drop is the source of seas
Don't think low of drop

LIBRARY

Good library mine
Sweet as bee hive boosts knowledge
Spreads glow all around

Groping in the dark
Good library shows you light
Books for better looks

Come to treasure land
Swim in oceans of learning
Library new world

Visit the library
Wander in realms of knowledge
Grow rich by learning

Clowns

Clowns Clowns everywhere
We dere not call ourselves clowns
But we laugh at clowns

We praise clowns in plays
Can not play the clown at times
Clown- a better doctor

Deserts, hills and seas
We pass them all with a smile
When clowns cling to us

Even crowns like clowns
As lotus blooms in moon lights
Reaps smiles in tensions

SPAM

Spam guard we all need
To check our thoughts and deeds
And generate values

Past gone post man's time
e-mails sail our day as seen
Spam guard saves your mail.

Gone are mail bombs days
Virus clings to mails and spoil
Check the spam daily

Hail to the e-mail
Male or female have their mail
Safe with spam guard on

COFFEE

Sunrise makes a morn
A sip of coffee gives joy
In our varied moods

Coffee frees us all
From dull and deep state in life
Each sip a new tide

Coffee in the morn
Drenches parched veins like rain
Aroma is left

Coffee like trophy
In hand remains for a while
A prized possession

MONEY

Man lives in money
By money and for money
But not off money

      East, West, North or South
      Money makes many things
      Contentment is rare

            Local or Global
            Without money no life at all
            Wealth omnipotent

                  Money to many
                  Soothing balm for poverty
                  From birth to death

SILENCE

Silence is violent
Like calm before storm on seas
Disturbs mental peace

Utter soothing words
Like Autumn winds give relief
Heals many traumas

Parched hearts need kind words
Like farm lands wait for showers
People crave for praise

All rainbow colours
Bloom full in your life slowly
Hopes rise in future

Positive Thinking

Positive approach
Like spring season rouses hope
Life is interesting

     The dark holds terrors
     Like creepers cling to our mind
     Knowledge gives us strength

          Dream well in your life
          Rainbows come within your reach
          Rare becomes common

               The days of future
               Like candles on Christmas eve
               Glow with happiness

MEMORY

All our memories
Pages written by our age
Witness of the past

> All bad memories
> Herbingers of restlessness
> Breads fears and tensions

> All good memories
> Mines of mirth sprinkles joy and
> Happiness in minds

> Life a heavy tale
> Woven out of memories
> With no boundaries

HEART

Hearts bruise easily
Tackle them with care is a feat
To all near and dear

All broken young hearts
Lands smashed by thunder storm
To gain strength is hard

Heart-a seat of love
Like honey in the beehive
Sweet in all ages

All strong emotions
Like hot winds in March month
Torture tender heart

DANCE

Learn to dance to the
Tunes of the people round you
For mental fitness

Dance of emotions
Sprouts so many tiffs and strifes
Made us play sad tunes

Siva's cosmic dance
Contains life and death in brief
Mild and wild fuse well

Our life a grand dance
Choreographed by Almighty
Aiming towards death

MIDNIGHT

Gives solace to all
Keeps every one in the deep sleep
With it's quite, calm lull

In the lap of sleep
Unperturbed by outer world
Wants to forget worries

Clock chimes at midnight
Strangles the midnight gently
Sprouts again next day

A friend to black deeds
Nourishes many dark acts
Chum to Marlowes

OLYMPICS

Dream of Olympics
Like farmers' dream of harvest
Best is put to test

Heart throbs for medals
As dying plants crave for water
Practice makes men win

Records break and roll
As sea tides lash at the shore
Sports men's testing ground

Some are born to win
Like lion hunting animals
Clash of Titans fine

DELHI VISIT

Sitting on the first seat
With friends and colleagues
Roaming in Delhi

There stood three flames
Reminding of patriots
'India Gate' Delhi

A group of soldiers
Presenting floral tributes
With solemn faces

Busy Delhi roads
Countless cars like waves on roads
Seasons bring no change

Wonderful structure
The Lotus Bahai Temple
Calm cool and serene

Grand Lotus Temple
Silence creeps into our hearts
Transformed souls come out

Grand Qutub Minar
Beckons all generations
Injects past gently

Recalled old memories
Amidst the old Monuments
Replicas of past

Pure iron pillar
Braving the changes of time
Man's creation great

Crumbling old stone walls
Sing sad songs of past glory
Mute in photographs

Best of India mall
Displays the works of art
Feast to foreign eyes

Time made lively past
Mute objects in museum
Symbol of splendour

Photo gallery
Opened new vistas of past
Age no bar to feel

People throng to see
Old and New tombs in Delhi
All throughout the year

Lord Hanumanji
A titan in Delhi stood
Filled us with wonder

Lakshmi Narayan
Marble temple a marvel
With lively idols

Masala mixture
At noon with onion and nuts
Tasty but spicy

Red Fort on Ring road
Brings to our minds Kings and Queens
Beyond mysteries

Plates full of fruit chat
Behind the shrine of Ganesh
Filled our eyes and stomach

Visited Raj Ghat
Tombs amidst stretches of lawns
Glorious Delhi